Reading for Main Ideas and Details in Informational Text
Grade 5

Table of Contents

Free Video Tutorial

 Use this QR code to launch a short video that provides instruction for skills featured in this book. To access the video from your smartphone or tablet:

- Download a free QR code scanner from your device's app store.
- Launch the scanning app on your device.
- Scan the code to visit the web page for this book.
- Find the video under the Resources tab.

This *Spectrum Focus* video is also available at:
- http://www.carsondellosa.com/704911
- www.youtube.com/user/CarsonDellosaPub

Spectrum®
An imprint of Carson-Dellosa Publishing LLC
P.O. Box 35665
Greensboro, NC 27425

ISBN 978-1-4838-2428-4

01-204157784

Focus On Reading for Main Ideas and Details

The ability to understand informational texts is an essential skill. Our world is full of nonfiction texts, including articles, websites, manuals, directions, maps, charts, and many more. Readers of these texts can use strategies to increase comprehension. These include answering questions by quoting evidence from the text and by inferring what is not directly stated, finding main ideas and the details that support them, summarizing, and explaining relationships between ideas. For each of these skills, *Reading for Main Ideas and Details in Informational Text* provides step-by-step teaching, explanations, and practice. Close reading of short nonfiction passages is followed by text-based comprehension questions that build critical-thinking skills.

Read this text closely. It will be used to illustrate the topics that follow.

The Ancestral Pueblo People

1   One prehistoric civilization of the southwestern United States was the Ancestral Puebloans. No one knows what they called themselves. Some archaeologists and scholars have called them the *Anasazi*. *Anasazi* is a Navajo word that means "ancient enemy." Over time, it came to mean "ancient people."

2   The Ancestral Puebloans came to the Southwest around 100 BC. They built simple homes with sticks and mud in shallow caves along canyon walls. They relied on foods they grew themselves, such as corn and squash. Because they were expert basket weavers, the first phase of their civilization is called the *Early Basket Maker Period*. This period lasted until around AD 500.

3   The next phase is the *Modified Basket Maker Period*. The people at this time wanted to be closer to their crops, so they built partially-underground homes in open areas near their farms. They still made baskets, but they also began making clay pots. Beans became an important crop because they could now be cooked over fires in clay pots. People began wearing turquoise jewelry and using bows and arrows for hunting.

4   The civilization's third phase, the *Developmental Pueblo Period*, began around AD 700. Homes were above ground, but kivas, or ceremonial rooms, were built partially underground. Now, people

made pottery for two purposes: cooking and beauty.

5   The *Great Pueblo Period* began around AD 1050. During this time, the people built the famous stone cliff dwellings called *pueblos* that resembled modern apartment buildings. Ladders were used to get to the upper stories. These ladders could be pulled inside to keep enemies out. Groups of cliff dwellings formed large communities. Trade with nearby tribes began.

6   Scholars are not sure what happened to the Ancestral Puebloans. Some believe they were victims of a drought. Others think that wars with other tribes were responsible for their disappearance. For whatever reason, by AD 1540, only three major pueblo clusters remained occupied.

Quoting from a Text to Answer Questions

Readers often answer questions about a text to show that they understand what it says. You may need to answer questions like these during a class discussion, for homework, or on a test.

Most questions can be answered by closely reading exactly what the text says. To answer some questions, readers will need to compare one part of the text to another part. When you answer a question, it is a good idea to include a direct quotation of evidence from the text. Quoting from the text will help you make sure that your answer matches what the text actually says.

Give your answer in three parts. First, answer the question in your own words. Then, quote evidence from the text that supports your answer. Finally, explain how the evidence makes the answer clear. Look at these examples of questions and answers about "The Ancestral Pueblo People." Notice how quotation marks, commas, and capital letters are used in quotations.

Question: Did the Ancestral Puebloans have enemies?
Answer: There are some reasons to believe that the Ancestral Puebloans had enemies. The text states that *Anasazi* once meant "ancient enemy" and that the civilization might have disappeared because of "wars with other tribes." The original name *Anasazi* might have come from people who considered the Ancestral Puebloans to be enemies. The tribes they fought against would have been enemies.

Question: How did the Ancestral Puebloans view clay pots differently in AD 600 and in AD 800?

Answer: In the early part of their civilization, the Ancestral Puebloans made pots for cooking and other practical purposes, but later they made pots that were works of art. According to the text, in AD 600, clay pots were made for cooking beans. By AD 800, pots were made for two purposes, "cooking and beauty." As time went on, pottery became a form of artwork for the Ancestral Puebloans.

Quoting from a Text to Draw Inferences

The answers to some questions cannot be found directly in the text. To arrive at an answer, readers must use what they have read in addition to what they already know to fill in missing information. Answering a question in this way is called *drawing an inference.*

An *inference* is a conclusion based on evidence. When making an inference, first look at evidence from the text. Then, think about other sources of information. Evidence can come from personal experience, from other texts you have read, from general knowledge about the world, and from logical thinking. Putting all this evidence together will help you draw good inferences.

When drawing an inference, it is a good idea to include a direct quotation of evidence from the text as well as an explanation of other evidence you use. Look at examples of inferences related to the text on page 2.

Question: Why don't scholars know for sure how the Ancestral Puebloans died out?

Inference: The Ancestral Puebloans had mostly disappeared by AD 1540. That was about 500 years ago. Scholars think they might have died out because they were "victims of a drought" or as a result of "wars with other tribes." I know that very little can survive for 500 years. Scholars may find clues, such as bits of clay pots and weapons, but not enough evidence to prove why the people disappeared. It was too long ago.

Question: Did the Ancestral Puebloans become more open to attack through their history?

Inference: Yes. Early homes were in protected places, in caves or partially underground. By the Great Pueblo Period, homes were in tall structures that "resembled modern apartment buildings." They needed ladders that could be pulled up to keep enemies out. By this time, the Ancestral Puebloans were also trading with other tribes. I know that living above ground and trading with others is riskier than staying underground and not trading. As time went on, the people opened themselves up to attack.

Focus On Reading for Main Ideas and Details

Finding Main Ideas and Key Details

The main ideas of an informational text are the most important ideas an author wants readers to understand and remember. Key details help to explain or *support* the main ideas. Without supporting details, readers may not fully understand the main ideas. Or, they may decide that not enough evidence is given to prove that the main ideas are true and believable.

Sometimes, a main idea is clearly stated near the beginning or ending of an informational text. In other informational texts, main ideas must be inferred from the details presented. Look at main ideas that can be inferred from "The Ancestral Pueblo People" and key details that support each one. Do you think there are enough key details given in the text to support each main idea?

Main Idea: **Over time, the Ancestral Puebloans became experts at making buildings from mud and stone.**
Key Detail: Early homes were simple, built from mud and sticks in shallow caves.
Key Detail: Later, homes were built only partially underground.
Key Detail: The Ancestral Puebloans are best known for the tall stone pueblo buildings resembling modern apartment buildings that they built into the sides of cliffs toward the end of their civilization.
Main Idea: **The Modified Basket Maker Period was a time of invention and change.**
Key Detail: The people began to build homes in open areas near farms.
Key Detail: They began making clay pots to use for cooking one of their crops, beans.
Key Detail: They wore turquoise jewelry and used bows and arrows for hunting.

Finding Relationships Between People, Events, and Ideas

Informational texts may explain historical events, scientific concepts, or technical procedures. The author connects details in a logical order so that main ideas become clear. One important way to understand informational texts is to pay attention to these connections. Look for relationships and interactions between people, events, and ideas.

Time lines, Venn diagrams, idea webs, and other graphic organizers can help show the connections between ideas in informational texts.

Focus On Reading for Main Ideas and Details

Look at the organizers below. They help make sense of information from "The Ancestral Pueblo People."

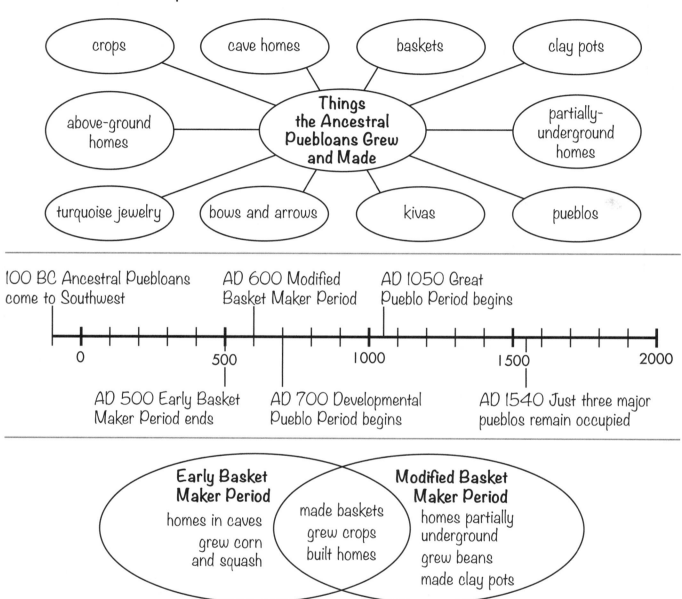

Summarizing a Text

Summarizing is a skill that most people use every day. When someone asks how your day was, you usually don't list every little thing that happened. Instead, you give a summary of the day's most important or interesting events. You probably do the same thing when you give a recap of a movie, book, or sporting event. A good

Focus On Reading for Main Ideas and Details

summary gives the "gist" of the text. It includes the main points and key details that are worth remembering. It leaves out less important details.

Readers are often asked to summarize what they read in informational texts. Good readers keep a running summary in their heads as they read, making a mental note when they read information that seems especially important or interesting. Written summaries are often required for homework and tests.

To write a summary, first use the five **W**s and **H** to ask questions about a text. Look at these example questions and answers about the text on page 2.

Who is the text about?	It is about the Ancestral Puebloan civilization.
What information is most important?	The history of the civilization can be divided into four periods: Early Basket Maker, Modified Basket Maker, Developmental Pueblo, and Great Pueblo.
When does something important happen?	The civilization lasted over 1,500 years, from 100 BC to AD 1540.
Where does something important happen?	The civilization flourished in the southwestern United States.
Why is this topic important?	This topic is important because it tells the history of a fascinating and mysterious prehistoric civilization.
How does the author explain the main ideas?	The author explains the main ideas by describing each period in the history of the Ancestral Puebloans.

The answers to these questions provide important information to include in a summary. A summary of a short passage like the one on page 2 should be about one paragraph (or three to five sentences) long. Read the example summary below.

"The Ancestral Pueblo People" tells the story of the prehistoric civilization that flourished in the southwestern United States for over 1,500 years. The history of the Ancestral Puebloans is divided into four periods: Early Basket Maker, Modified Basket Maker, Developmental Pueblo, and Great Pueblo. Over time, the Ancestral Puebloans changed from people who lived in caves and made baskets to people who built huge pueblos that looked like modern apartment buildings. No one knows why they disappeared, but the facts we do know about them are fascinating.

Informational Text Quoting from a Text

Read the text. Use it to answer the questions on pages 9 and 10.

Tiny but Tough

1   If you imagined the hardiest animal on the planet, what would it be? A large or fierce animal, like a great blue whale or a lion? Or something smaller, like a rat or a cockroach? You might be surprised to find out that the toughest living animal is the tardigrade. This tiny creature measures only about one millimeter in length. Yet it amazes scientists with its ability to survive almost anything.

2   Tardigrades are also known as *water bears*. These microscopic animals have eight legs, claws, and pudgy faces with lots of folds. Tardigrades are ancient. Fossils of tardigrades date them at 500 million years old. It's not surprising that this little creature is still alive today. It seems that tardigrades are nearly indestructible!

3   One of the most amazing things about tardigrades is that they can survive years without water. All animal life needs water to survive. This is true for tardigrades, too, but they are able to go without it for long periods of time. Without water, they go into a sort of hibernation. Scientists know for sure that they can be brought back to life after eight years without water. In 1948, an Italian scientist said she brought some back to life from a 120-year-old sample of moss. No one else has found this same result, but it doesn't seem impossible.

4   Tardigrades can also live in extreme temperatures. They have been found in icy Antarctica as well as in steamy Japanese hot springs. Tardigrades have survived being heated to temperatures of more than 300°F for 15 minutes and being frozen at about −450°F.

5   Tardigrades aren't just hardy creatures on Earth. They can survive a trip to space and back. If humans went into space without protection, they would die. However, in 2007, tardigrades were attached to a satellite that was sent into space. When it returned to Earth, many of the tardigrades were still alive. Some of the females had laid eggs. Even the babies were in good shape.

6   Although tardigrades can live in extreme places, most do not. In fact, they tend to lead rather quiet lives in or near water. Some suck the juice from moss or lichen; others are carnivorous. There is still a lot for scientists to learn about these interesting creatures, but that shouldn't be a problem. Tardigrades appear to be here to stay!

NAME _____

Guided Practice Quoting from a Text

1. Can tardigrades survive without water?

> Details in "Tiny but Tough" help you answer this question. To show that your answer is supported by evidence, use a quotation from the text in your answer. Write your answer in three parts. First, answer in your own words. Then, strengthen your answer by quoting evidence from the text. Finally, relate the evidence back to your answer.

First, answer question #1 in your own words.

_____

Next, quote evidence from the text. Use quotation marks around exact words from the text.

_____

Finally, tell how the evidence you quoted supports your answer.

_____

2. How big are tardigrades?

> Quote evidence from two different places in the text to answer this question. Write your answer in three parts. Make sure to punctuate quotations correctly. Study the guidelines below.

The text states, "Tardigrades are ancient."

The tag is followed by a comma.

If the quotation is a complete sentence, begin it with a capital letter.

The ending punctuation mark goes inside of the quotation marks.

Quote evidence from the text to answer question #2.

_____

_____

_____

_____

NAME _____

Independent Practice Quoting from a Text

Draw a line from each question to evidence from the text that you might quote in your answer.

1. What do tardigrades eat?

2. How long can tardigrades survive without water?

3. Where do most tardigrades live?

4. How old are tardigrades?

Fossils of tardigrades date them at 500 million years old.

They tend to lead rather quiet lives in or near water.

They can survive years without water.

Some suck the juice from moss or lichen; others are carnivorous.

Quote evidence from the text to answer each question. Write answers in three parts.

5. Can tardigrades survive in space?

_____

_____

_____

6. What do tardigrades look like?

_____

_____

_____

7. Why are tardigrades nearly indestuctible?

_____

_____

_____

Informational Text Drawing Inferences

Read the text. Use it to answer the questions on pages 12 and 13.

The Unsinkable Ship

1   In April of 1912, the *Titanic* set sail from England. The enormous vessel was bound for New York, but it never made it there. The *Titanic* hit an iceberg off the coast of Newfoundland. A giant gash was torn in the side of the ship, and it sank. The *Titanic*, once called "the unsinkable ship," had only one voyage. Today, it rests on the ocean floor.

2   At the time, the *Titanic* was the largest moving object on Earth—about three football fields long and as tall as a 17-story building. The giant ship had everything a person might need, including elevators, a swimming pool, libraries, and barber shops. The ship's creators had thought of everything. Everything, that is, except enough lifeboats for all the passengers.

3   About 2,200 people set sail on the *Titanic*. Many rich and powerful people were onboard. They were looking forward to a one-of-a-kind experience. The ship was one of the first to have electric lights and telephones in the rooms. In today's money, the most expensive tickets would cost nearly $100,000!

4   Late at night on April 14, the boat hit an iceberg. The ship's wall suffered a 300-foot tear. Water gushed into the hulls. There were only 16 lifeboats on the *Titanic*. Each could hold 65 people, but most of the boats were not filled during the disaster. Even if they had been, many would still have died. There were just not enough lifeboats to hold all the passengers and crew.

5   Three hours after the *Titanic* hit the iceberg, it sank. The great ship dropped almost two and a half miles before it came to rest on the ocean floor. Because people thought that the boat could not sink, many did not take the accident seriously at first. In fact, the orchestra continued to play as the boat sank!

6   More than 1,500 people died. The news stunned the world. It was hard to believe that such a grand ship and so many of her passengers were gone. Although treasure seekers spent years looking for the wreck of the *Titanic*, it was not found until 1985. Today, the remains of the boat are still at the bottom of the ocean. Some of the artifacts, though, are on exhibit. They help people remember those who were lost and bring their stories to life.

Guided Practice Drawing Inferences

1. Why were tickets to travel on the *Titanic* so expensive?

> The answer to this question cannot be found directly in the text. However, evidence in the text will help you arrive at an answer. "The Unsinkable Ship" describes how large the ship was and how many new, fancy things it had onboard. Quote some of this evidence in your answer. Then, think about your own experience. Do new, fancy things (like a new electronic game system) and new experiences (like a new amusement park) tend to be expensive? Why? How can you use logical thinking to answer the question?

Draw an inference to answer the question. Quote evidence from the text.

_____

_____

_____

_____

2. What did treasure seekers hope to find in the wreck of the *Titanic*?

> Before drawing an inference, think about information contained in the question, information found in the text, and information from your own experience. The question mentions "treasure seekers." What kinds of treasure might have been on the *Titanic* when it sank? Evidence from the text tells you what kinds of things and people were on the ship. What might the passengers have carried that could be called *treasure*?

Draw an inference to answer the question. Quote evidence from the text.

_____

_____

_____

_____

Independent Practice Drawing Inferences

For each item, consider the evidence listed. Use it to draw an inference.

1. Why did rich and powerful people want to sail on the *Titanic's* first voyage?
   - The text says that rich and powerful people "were looking forward to a one-of-a-kind experience."
   - The text says that the new ship was the largest moving object on Earth and that it had electric lights, phones, libraries, elevators, and more.
   - Rich and powerful people can afford to buy new, fancy things. They can afford to be the first to do something new and exciting.

   _____

   _____

   _____

2. Why did people need to sail on the *Titanic* to cross the Atlantic Ocean in 1912?
   - The text says the ship was "bound for New York."
   - The Atlantic Ocean lies between England and New York.
   - Today, most people cross the ocean in airplanes.
   - Flying in an airplane was not available to most people until the 1940s.

   _____

   _____

   _____

3. Why did the designers of the *Titanic* fail to include enough lifeboats for all the passengers? Quote evidence from the text in your answer.

   _____

   _____

   _____

   _____

Informational Text Main Ideas and Key Details

Read the text. Use it to answer the questions on pages 15 and 16.

Saving the Monarchs

1   The oyamel fir tree is quivering like a living animal. It is hard to tell where the tree itself is and why it looks so odd. It is the winter home of monarch butterflies. More than 10,000 butterflies can roost in a single tree! The creatures may have traveled 3,000 miles to get here.

2   Monarchs are one of the most well-known types of butterflies in the U.S. They are easy to recognize by their orange and black markings. Sadly, their days here may be numbered. In 1996, there were more than one billion monarchs in the U.S. Today, that number has dropped by about 90 percent. Human actions have taken their toll on this delicate insect. To save them, we need to make changes to protect their habitat. The good news is that in 2015, the U.S. Fish and Wildlife Service pledged $3.2 million to help monarchs.

3   Monarchs migrate each winter. Monarchs in the northern U.S. migrate to Florida and Mexico. They can fly 50 to 100 miles per day. The farthest a monarch was recorded flying in a day was 265 miles! This is an amazing feat for a tiny creature that weighs less than a paperclip. Not only can monarchs fly great distances, they know where to go. Monarchs from all over the northern U.S. end up in the same parts of Mexico.

4   One hardship for monarchs is the loss of habitat. Logging takes away roosts. It can even change the temperature of a forest. Thinner forests mean cooler temperatures. A monarch's body needs to be at least 86° F to fly. Farmers also add to the problem. Many spray their crops with *herbicides*, or poisons that kill weeds. At the same time, they also kill the milkweed plant. Monarchs need milkweed to survive. Monarch caterpillars eat only milkweed leaves. Adults lay eggs on the milkweed plant, too.

5   Although monarchs are in danger, humans can help. Farmers, scientists, and communities must work together. Gardeners can plant milkweed and pollinator plants. Forests can be protected. People can support groups that help monarchs. Humans have created the problems that face monarchs today. It is our job to solve those problems and protect these beautiful butterflies.

Guided Practice Main Ideas and Key Details

1. What third detail from "Saving the Monarchs" supports the main idea shown below?

Main Idea: Human actions are threatening monarchs' habitats.

Key Detail: Logging takes away roosts for monarchs.

Key Detail: Herbicides kill the milkweed plant that monarchs depend on.

Key Detail: _____

> Details in informational texts can support more than one main idea. A main idea is only true if it is supported by strong key details. A main idea may not be true if there is not enough evidence in the text to support it. Look at the main idea above. Details that support it must describe human actions and tell how exactly how they are harming things in nature that a monarch needs (or its habitat). Scan the text on page 14. Can you find another supporting detail for this main idea? Is this main idea well-supported by key details?

Now, write a key detail from the text on the line above to answer question #1.

2. What main idea about monarchs' flying ability is supported by the text?

> The question asks you to write a main idea that is supported by key details in the text. What details can you find on page 14 about how well or how far monarchs fly? Details in the text talk about how much monarchs weigh, what their migration patterns are, and how far they have been known to fly in a single day. Looking at all these details, what main idea can you write that sums up the evidence? It could be something as simple as "Monarchs can fly great distances." It could express an opinion such as "Monarchs are amazing flyers." Decide how strong or specific the main idea should be based on the key details you find.

Write a main idea to answer question #2.

_____

_____

Independent Practice Main Ideas and Key Details

Read the main ideas below. Write one above each set of matching key details.

- Monarchs are a threatened species.
- Many people know about monarch butterflies and want to help them.
- Humans can help protect monarchs.

1. Main Idea: _____

Key Detail: Gardeners can plant milkweed plants.

Key Detail: People can help protect forests.

2. Main Idea: _____

Key Detail: The population of monarchs in the U.S. has dropped 90% since 1996.

Key Detail: Monarchs have a hard time finding the milkweed plants they need.

3. Main Idea: _____

Key Detail: Monarchs are easy to recognize by their orange and black markings.

Key Detail: The U.S. Fish and Wildlife Service pledged $3.2 million to help monarchs.

4. Write a check mark beside main ideas that are well-supported by key details in the text on page 14. Write an *X* beside main ideas that are not supported by key details.

_____ There are many ways that people can help monarchs.

_____ Now that people are helping monarchs, their population is on the rise.

_____ Loggers care a great deal about monarchs.

_____ The milkweed plant is an important part of the monarchs' habitat.

5. Write three key details from the text on page 14 that support the main idea.

Main Idea: Monarchs are delicate insects.

Key Detail: _____

Key Detail: _____

Key Detail: _____

Informational Text People and Events

Read the text. Use it to answer the questions on pages 18 and 19.

A Man of the People

1   In 1869, Mohandas Gandhi was born in India. He was a shy child and an average student. He married at the age of 13, which was typical for the time. In most respects, he was ordinary. There was little about Gandhi's early life that predicted the impact he would have on the world.

2   Gandhi studied law and world religions. He was a Hindu, but he was curious about other religions. After finishing school, Gandhi moved to South Africa in 1893. It was hard to leave his family, but he needed to find work.

3   Gandhi was bothered by the segregation he saw in South Africa. *Segregation* means "keeping people separated based on race or religion." Segregation in South Africa reminded Gandhi of the way some people were treated in India. There, the *caste system* was strong. People in higher castes had more money, respect, and power. People in the lowest castes were poor. They led hard lives and were treated badly. Gandhi wanted to help all Indians, no matter their class or caste.

4   In 1896, Gandhi's wife and sons came to South Africa. Gandhi began a group called the Phoenix Settlement. Its people lived and farmed together. They were equal and shared what they had. Their goal was to live simply and peacefully.

5   In 1906, Gandhi invented the idea *satyagraha*, which means "truth force." He and his followers protested things they found unjust. They did not become angry. They did not fight back. Gandhi believed that this form of protest would result in a peaceful solution. He and other protesters were beaten or sent to jail over the years, but Gandhi held firm to his beliefs.

6   Gandhi finally came home to India in 1915. There, he continued to work for peace and justice. Many of his efforts were to help India gain independence from British rule. He was sent to prison again and again, but India finally won independence in 1947.

7   Less than a year later, in 1948, Gandhi was assassinated. He had spent his life working for peace, so it seemed very wrong that he should die this way. Gandhi was a force for good in the world. He inspired many leaders who followed him. "Be the change that you wish to see in the world," Gandhi said. No one could be a better example of this than he was.

Guided Practice People and Events

1. What would people who lived in the Phoenix Settlement say about the caste system in India? Base your answer on evidence from the text on page 17.

> To answer this question, look for details in the text about the two groups or systems being compared—the Phoenix Settlement and the Indian caste system. How are they alike and different? What does each value? Before writing your answer, it may help to make lists like the ones below.

Phoenix Settlement
People live together.
People share what they have.
Goal is simple living.

Indian Caste System
People divided into different groups, or castes.
Some castes are rich, and others are poor.
Makes life hard for some castes.

Now, use evidence from the text to answer the question.

_____

_____

_____

2. What happened in Gandhi's life in 1906? What was one effect of this event?

> Some questions ask you to think about historical events. To answer, read the text closely to find dates, events, and cause-and-effect relationships. To answer this question, search for the date 1906. Since the text is arranged in time order beginning in 1869 and ending in 1948, you know that a description of what happened in 1906 will be somewhere in the middle. Read that part carefully. Then, scan the events that came after. Which of these was an effect of the event in 1906? Why are the two events related?

Now, use evidence from the text to answer the question.

_____

_____

_____

Independent Practice People and Events

1. Compare and contrast Gandhi's early life (1869–1895) and his later life (1896–1948). On each side of the Venn diagram, write words and phrases from the text that describe Gandhi during each period. In the center of the Venn diagram, write words and phrases that describe his entire life. On the lines below the diagram, write about how Gandhi changed over his lifetime and how he remained the same.

Gandhi's Life

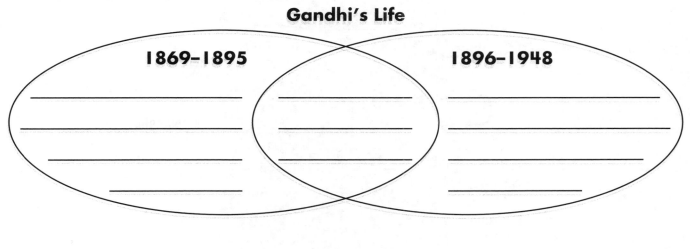

2. Complete the time line with events from Gandhi's life described in "A Man of the People." Then, on the lines below, write about one event. Tell how the event helps to explain why Gandhi is such an inspiring and well-loved person from history.

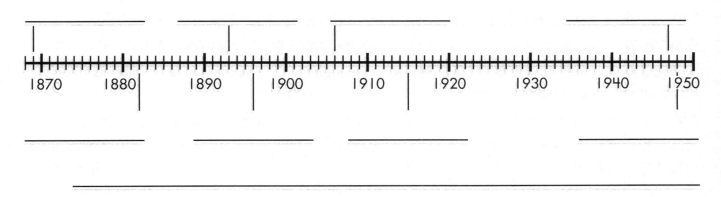

Informational Text Related Ideas

Read the text. Use it to answer the questions on pages 21 and 22.

The Human Heart

[1] The heart has four **chambers**, or areas: the left and right **ventricles** and the left and right **atriums**.

[2] The heart's four **valves** (mitral, aortic, pulmonary, and tricuspid) make sure that the blood flows only in the direction it is supposed to go.

[3] Blood that leaves the heart is carried through **arteries**. The aorta and the pulmonary arteries are the two main arteries carrying blood *away* from the heart.

[4] Blood is carried toward the heart through **veins**. The superior and inferior vena cava and the pulmonary veins carry blood *to* the heart.

[5] When the heart beats, the muscle contracts. The ventricles squeeze blood out through the arteries, where it is carried to the rest of the body. Meanwhile, the left and right atriums refill with blood from the lungs and body that returns to the heart through the veins. The heart relaxes, and blood is dumped into the ventricles to begin the cycle again.

Guided Practice Related Ideas

1. What happens after the left and right atriums fill with blood?

In order to answer a question about how something works, you need a good general understanding of a text and any charts, graphs, or diagrams that go along with it. You may need to read a text several times in order to really understand it. Be an active reader by using your imagination to picture events happening as you read. It may help to draw your own illustration or to restate ideas in your own words. Reread the text on page 20. Each time a part of the heart is described, point to it in the diagram. Then, read the text again. This time, use your finger to trace the flow of blood through the diagram of the heart. Now, the question should be easier to answer.

Answer question #1 in your own words.

_____

_____

_____

2. Where does blood go when it leaves the heart?

To answer this question, scan the text to find out which structures carry blood away from the heart. Find those parts in the diagram. Then, keep reading to find out where these structures take the blood. Look at the diagram and imagine the living heart beating inside your body. Where does blood go when it flows away from your heart through the arteries?

Now, answer question #2 in your own words.

_____

_____

_____

Independent Practice Related Ideas

1. Number the steps 1–4 to show the order in which events happen as blood is carried away from the heart. Use the text to help you.

   ____ The aorta and pulmonary arteries carry blood to the rest of the body.

   ____ The heart muscle contracts (squeezes, becomes smaller, or beats).

   ____ The pulmonary valve and aortic valve shut to keep blood flowing in the right direction, away from the heart.

   ____ The left and right ventricles push blood into the pulmonary artery and aorta.

2. Number the steps 1–4 to show the order in which events happen as blood flows into the heart. Use the text to help you.

   ____ The heart relaxes. Blood is dumped from the left and right atriums into the left and right ventricles.

   ____ The superior vena cava, inferior vena cava, and pulmonary veins carry blood from the lungs and body into the heart.

   ____ The left and right atriums fill with blood.

   ____ The tricuspid valve and mitral valve shut to keep blood flowing in the right direction, into the heart.

3. Exercise makes muscles in your body bigger, stronger, and more flexible. The heart is a muscle. Explain how exercise can help your heart work well.

   _____

   _____

   _____

4. Exercise and a healthy diet keep your heart healthy. In unhealthy hearts, a substance called *plaque* can build up on artery walls, making the opening inside the tube narrower. How might narrow arteries affect the way the heart works? Use the text and diagram on page 20 to help you.

   _____

   _____

   _____

Informational Text Summarizing

Read the text. Use it to answer the questions below and on page 24.

Look Out for Viruses!

1   You've probably had a biological virus before. It's a germ, like the common cold, that makes you feel lousy. A computer virus is similar. It isn't a germ, but it can affect the way a computer works.

2   A computer virus can delete data on your computer. Like a germ, it spreads easily. A bad computer virus can even erase everything on your hard drive!

3   The good news is that protection programs work well. Anti-virus software installed on your computer checks regularly for viruses. It alerts you if it finds one. It's important to make sure you have the latest software updates. New viruses pop up all the time. Your computer has to know what to look for in order to protect you.

4   Another way to protect yourself is to be careful about files you open. If you see an attachment you did not expect, do not open it. Viruses can be disguised as documents, photos, or videos. You can protect yourself from nasty germs by washing your hands. Good habits can protect you from computer viruses, too!

Guided Practice Summarizing

A summary includes the most important information from a text. To find the most important information, complete the chart with evidence from the text.

Who or what is the text about?	1. _____
What information is most important?	Computer viruses can cause harm by deleting data.
When does something important happen?	Computer viruses are changing all the time, and can strike a computer at any time.
Where does something important happen?	2. _____
Why is this topic important?	3. _____
How does something important happen?	Computer viruses can get into your computer disguised as files. Anti-virus software protects your computer.

Independent Practice Summarizing

1. On the lines below, write a summary of "Look Out for Viruses!" Write in complete sentences using your own words. Use the completed chart on page 23 to help you. Include only the most important information from the text. Leave out less important details. Your summary should be short—use only the lines provided below.

_____

_____

_____

_____

_____

_____

2. Reread the summary you wrote. Did you include only the most important information? On the lines below, explain why or why not. If you included non-important details in your summary, cross them out.

_____

_____

_____

3. Now, compare your summary to the completed chart on page 23. Did you include all the information from the chart in your summary? On the lines below, explain why or why not. If you need to, add more information to the summary you wrote above.

_____

_____

_____

Performance Task

Read the texts. Use them to complete each step of the task that follows.

Weather Balloons

[1]   Weather balloons are released twice a day, every day of they year, from about 900 places around the world and reach average heights of 62,000 to 105,000 feet. A device called a *radiosonde* is attached to each balloon. It sends data back to the ground every few seconds.

[2]   Weather balloons provide data about wind, air pressure, temperature, and humidity. This information helps meteorologists predict what kind of weather is headed our way. If you find a radiosonde, look for a mailing bag and instructions. If you return it to the National Weather Service, it can be fixed and reused!

Weather Satellites

[1]   Weather satellites help predict the weather. There are two main types. Geostationary operational environmental satellites (GOES) hover over the equator about 22,000 miles above Earth. They move at the same speed that our planet rotates. That way, they capture data from the same area.

[2]   The other type is a polar-orbiting satellite. It is much closer—about 500 miles above Earth. Its orbit passes over the North and South Poles and covers a much larger area. The data that the two types of satellites send back to Earth give a complete picture. It helps track storms and cloud patterns and measure winds. The satellite images you see on the news were created by weather satellites.

Weather Radar

[1]   If you've ever watched a weather forecast on the news, you've probably heard the term *Doppler radar*. This tool is based on the Doppler effect. Think of the sound of a train whistle. As it gets closer to you, the pitch changes. It sounds different as it reaches and then passes you. There is a change in the frequency of sound. It's called the *Doppler effect*.

[2]   Radar towers that stand about 150 feet tall send out radio waves. Some of the waves bounce off raindrops or snow crystals. Doppler radar measures the frequency of the returning radio waves. Computers convert this information into pictures that forecasters use to predict the weather.

Performance Task

1. What is the Doppler effect? Quote evidence from the text in your answer.

   _____

   _____

2. Why are meteorologists so interested in finding out what is happening in Earth's atmosphere? Quote evidence from the text in your answer.

   _____

   _____

3. Which main idea is supported by details in all three texts?
   A. Weather predictions are getting more accurate all the time.
   B. High-tech devices help meteorologists predict the weather.
   C. Earth's atmosphere is full of weather balloons.
   D. Meteorologists collect data about wind and cloud patterns.

4. Which key detail provides support for the main idea "Weather devices convert data into pictures that provide forecasting information"?
   A. Satellite images you see on the news were created by weather satellites.
   B. Radio waves bounce off raindrops or snow crystals.
   C. Weather balloons provide data about wind, air pressure, temperature, and humidity.
   D. Weather satellites help predict the weather.

5. What do meteorologists rely on most to help them do their jobs?
   A. weather balloons
   B. the National Weather Service
   C. data collected about Earth's atmosphere
   D. radar towers

Performance Task

6. Which sentence would not belong in a good summary of all three texts?

   A. Meteorologists use technology to gather data about the weather.

   B. Data about wind, air pressure, temperature, humidity, cloud patterns, and precipitation help predict the weather

   C. Weather data is converted into graphs and pictures that help us understand the weather.

   D. A change in the frequency of sound is called the *Doppler effect.*

7. Imagine that you have been asked to create a visual aid for your classmates that explains different types of devices that collect data about the weather. Your graphic should be clearly organized so that it is easy to take in at a glance. It should include all the information needed to help your classmates understand what each weather device is and how it works.

First, review the rubric below. Then, write information from the three texts in the spaces on page 28 to create your visual aid. On the lines at the bottom of the page, write a main idea for your graphic. If you wish, color your visual aid and add illustrations.

	Proficient	**Learning**	**Beginner**
Main Idea	A main idea is included which is supported by key details about each weather device.	A main idea is included which is supported by key details about some weather devices.	A main idea is not included.
Key Details	Key details from the texts are included for 4 weather devices.	Key details from the texts are included for 2–3 weather devices.	Key details from the texts are included for 0–1 weather devices.
Relationships Between Ideas	All 4 weather devices are in order according to height above Earth.	Only 2–3 weather devices are in order according to height above Earth.	Only 0–1 weather devices are in order according to height above Earth.

After completing your visual aid, use the rubric to evaluate your graphic. For each topic, circle *Proficient, Learning,* or *Beginner.* This will help you know what skills you need to work on.

NAME _____

Performance Task

Height above Earth: _____
Weather device: _____
How it works: _____
_____
Data collected: _____

Height above Earth: _____
Weather device: _____
How it works: _____
_____
Data collected: _____

Space Begins (62 miles)

Height above Earth: _____
Weather device: _____
How it works: _____
_____
Data collected: _____

Height above Earth: _____
Weather device: _____
How it works: _____
_____
Data collected: _____

Earth

Main Idea: _____

_____

Assessment

Read the text. Use it to answer the questions that follow.

When the City Shook

1   One of the worst natural disasters in U.S. history happened in San Francisco on April 18, 1906. At 5:12 A.M., the earth began to rumble and shake. Walls fell, bridges and roads collapsed, and trees were uprooted. Most people were asleep in bed. They had no warning. In less than a minute, their world began to crumble.

2   The earthquake was caused by a rupture along the San Andreas Fault line. The city of San Francisco lies along this fault, and it is still the source of earthquakes today. The 1906 quake measured about 7.8 on the Richter scale. It was so strong that tremors could be felt hundreds of miles away.

3   The earthquake was devastating. Vibrations were so strong that soil particles lost contact with one another. This caused the ground in some areas to behave like a liquid rather than a solid. Buildings sitting on this soil collapsed—there was nothing solid to support them.

4   The quake didn't last long, but it caused massive damage. The worst damage was caused by fire. Broken gas lines caused fires to break out all over the city. There were as many as 50 major fires in San Francisco in the days following the earthquake. Some were so large that they grew, spread, and joined with other fires. To make things worse, water lines were broken. This meant there was no way to get water to the fires.

5   Firefighters tried to set fire to some buildings on purpose. They wanted to create a *firebreak* so that the fires would burn out instead of spreading. This idea is often used when fighting forest fires. Unfortunately, the attempt was not successful. The firefighters tried to use dynamite, but they did not know how to use it properly. The fires burned for three days and nights. Nearly 30,000 buildings were destroyed.

6   In the end, about 3,000 people lost their lives as a result of the earthquake. San Francisco was nearly ruined. Over the next decade, the city was rebuilt. In many ways, the new city was better than before. It was well planned and structured. Although the great quake of 1906 happened more than a hundred years ago, San Franciscans have never forgotten it.

NAME _____

Assessment

Part 1: I can quote an informational text to answer questions.

1. What are two examples of the massive damage caused by the San Francisco earthquake of 1906? Quote evidence from the text in your answer.

_____

_____

2. Why are earthquakes a concern for people who live in San Francisco? Quote evidence from the text in your answer.

_____

_____

3. Complete the chart with data about the 1906 San Francisco quake.

Year	Time	Richter Scale Measurement	Buildings Destroyed	Lives Lost

Part 2: I can draw inferences.

1. Sometimes, good things come from bad. Describe at least two ways that the 1906 earthquake might have been a "blessing in disguise" for San Franciscans. Quote evidence from the text in your answer.

_____

_____

2. Why would San Franciscans today still think about the earthquake of 1906? Describe at least two reasons. Quote evidence from the text in your answer.

_____

_____

NAME _____

Assessment

Part 3: I can find main ideas and key details.

1. Write a main idea that is supported by the key details given.

   Main Idea: _____

   Key detail: Water lines were broken.

   Key detail: Firefighters could not put out the fires.

   Key detail: Bridges and roads collapsed.

2. Write key details from the text that support the main idea given.

   Main idea: The quake of 1906 caused massive damage to San Francisco.

   Key detail: _____

   Key detail: _____

   Key detail: _____

3. Which is not a main idea supported by details in "When the City Shook"?

   A. The San Francisco quake of 1906 was one of the worst natural disasters in U.S. history.

   B. Vibrations from the earthquake had devastating effects.

   C. City officials and services were unable to cope with the disaster.

   D. The earthquake of 1906 ruined the city of San Francisco.

Part 4: I can describe relationships between people, events, and ideas.

1. Fill in the chart. For each feature of San Francisco, describe at least one impact of the earthquake of 1906.

Roads and bridges	
Soil and trees	
Buildings	
City services	
People	

Assessment

2. People in San Francisco still face the threat of earthquakes. On the lines below, write three ideas for things they might do to help prepare for another massive earthquake. Base your ideas on evidence from the text.

- _____

- _____

- _____

Part 5: I can summarize an informational text.

Complete the chart with evidence from the text.

Who or what is the text about?	1. _____
What information is most important?	2. _____
When does something important happen?	3. _____
Where does something important happen?	4. _____
Why is this topic important?	5. _____
How does something important happen?	6. _____

7. On the lines below, write a summary of "When the City Shook" in your own words. Use your answers to items 1–6 to help you.

_____

_____

_____

_____

_____

_____

Answer Key

Page 9

1. Answers will vary. Possible answer: Yes. "Tiny but Tough" explains that without water, tardigrades "go into a sort of hibernation." They need water to live, but they can go without it for a long time. **2.** Answers will vary. Possible answer: Tardigrades are very small. The text calls them "microscopic" and describes them as being "about one millimeter in length." As the title of the text says, tardigrades are tiny but tough.

Page 10

1. Some suck the juice from moss or lichen; others are carnivorous. **2.** They can survive years without water. **3.** They tend to lead rather quiet lives in or near water. **4.** Fossils of tardigrades date them at 500 million years old. **5.** Answers will vary. Possible answer: Yes. "Tiny but Tough" explains that in 2007, "Tardigrades were attached to a satellite that was sent into space." Most of them were still alive when the satellite returned to Earth. Tardigrades can survive even the harsh environment of space. **6.** Answers will vary. Possible answer: Tardigrades are tiny creatures with an interesting appearance. The text describes them as having "eight legs, claws, and pudgy faces with lots of folds." Since they are called "water bears," they must resemble tiny bears. **7.** Tardigrades are nearly indestructible because they can live in harsh conditions without dying. The text states that they "can be brought back to life after eight years without water," that they "have

been found in icy Antarctica as well as in steamy Japanese hot springs," and that they have been to space and back. Tardigrades are hardy creatures that can survive almost anything!

Page 12

1. Answers will vary. Possible answer: Tickets for the *Titanic's* first voyage were probably very expensive for several reasons. First, the ship was new and had lots of amazing things onboard. The text explains, "The ship was one of the first to have electric lights and telephones in the rooms." The *Titanic* must have been very expensive to build, so the tickets would need to be expensive to pay for it. Second, the *Titanic* was new and exciting. Many people wanted to experience it, so the owners could charge a lot of money. **2.** Answers will vary. Possible answer: The *Titanic* was a modern ship in 1912. It contained many fine things such as libraries and elevators. Things from these areas might be worth money today, especially since they are now antiques. Also, the text explains that the *Titanic's* passengers included many "rich and powerful people." These passengers might have brought valuable items onboard, including money and jewelry. Some of these things would still be in the ship on the bottom of the ocean. Treasure seekers hoped to find antiques, money, jewelry, and other valuables on *Titanic's* wreck.

Answer Key

Page 13

1. Answers will vary. Possible answer: The text explains that rich and powerful people were "looking forward to a one-of-a-kind experience" on the *Titanic*. They probably wanted to use their money to be the first to sail on the ship and see and enjoy all the new things on the ship. **2.** Answers will vary. Possible answer: "The Unsinkable Ship" explains that *Titanic* was supposed to travel between England and New York. In 1912, sailing across the Atlantic Ocean was not just done for pleasure. Today, people cross the ocean by airplane, but air travel was not available to most people until after World War II. In 1912, people needed ships like *Titanic* to cross the Atlantic Ocean. **3.** Answers will vary. Possible answer: There were not enough lifeboats on *Titanic* to hold all 2,200 passengers. The text states, "People thought that the boat could not sink." This helps explain why the designers left out lifeboats. They were probably so busy designing fancy rooms on the boat that they forgot something basic such as lifeboats. They really believed the ship was unsinkable.

Page 15

1. Logging lowers the temperature of the forest, making it too cool for monarchs to reach the body temperature needed to be able to fly. **2.** Answers will vary. Possible answer: Monarchs are small and delicate, but they are amazing flyers.

Page 16

1. Humans can help protect monarchs.
2. Monarchs are a threatened species.
3. Many people know about monarchs and want to help them. **4.** Students should check the first and fourth ideas. Students should write *X* beside the second and third ideas.
5. Answers will vary. Possible answers: Monarchs weigh less than a paperclip. Monarch caterpillars eat only milkweed leaves. A monarch's body needs to be at least 86° F in order to fly.

Page 18

1. Answers will vary. Possible answer: People who lived in the Phoenix Settlement would say that the Indian caste system was wrong. Members believed that everyone was equal. They shared and lived simply. In the caste system, people were divided into groups. Some groups had a lot, and others had little. The Phoenix Settlement would say that the caste system was unfair and unjust.
2. Answers will vary. Possible answer: In 1906, Gandhi invented the idea satyagraha. This event affected the rest of Gandhi's life because it explained why he was driven to fight for justice. One effect is that Gandhi was beaten and sent to jail. If he had not become such a strong believer in satyagraha, this probably would not have happened.

Page 19

1. Answers will vary. Possible answers: 1869–1895, shy, average, ordinary, curious,

Answer Key

bothered by segregation; 1896–1948, believed in satyagraha, protested, beaten or sent to jail, held firm beliefs, helped India gain independence, assassinated, working for peace, inspired many leaders; Center, Indian, curious about other people, lived in South Africa and India, believed that segregation and the caste system were wrong; **2.** Students should write these events on the time line: 1869, Gandhi born; 1882, Gandhi marries; 1893, Gandhi moves to South Africa; 1896, Gandhi starts Phoenix Settlement; 1906, Gandhi invents satyagraha; 1915, Gandhi returns to India; 1947, India gains independence; 1948, Gandhi assassinated

Page 21

1. After the left and right atriums fill with blood, the heart relaxes and blood is dumped into the ventricles. The cycle begins again. Blood is carried out of the ventricles through arteries to the rest of the body. **2.** When blood leaves the heart through the arteries, it is carried to the lungs and the rest of the body.

Page 22

1. 4, 1, 3, 2; **2.** 3, 1, 2, 4; **3.** Exercise can make your heart bigger, stronger, and more flexible. A strong, healthy heart can do a better job of pumping blood through your body. **4.** If arteries are narrowed, less blood will be able to travel away from the heart to the rest of the body, and less blood will travel back to the heart through the veins. Your body parts may not have enough blood flowing

through them to work well.

Page 23

1. The text is about computer viruses. **2.** Viruses can get inside your computer and affect the way it works. **3.** This topic is important because everyone wants and needs protection from computer viruses.

Page 24

1. Summaries will vary. Possible summary: Computer viruses are a threat to everyone. They can enter your computer. Then, they delete data on your computer. It is important to use anti-virus software to protect your computer from viruses. **2.** Answers will vary. **3.** Answers will vary.

Performance Task

1. The Doppler effect happens when there is a change in the frequency of sound as something gets closer to you. The text explains, "It sounds different as it reaches and then passes you." Meteorologists look for the Doppler effect when radio waves bounce off raindrops or snow crystals. **2.** Weather events such as rain and snow are the result of conditions in Earth's atmosphere. The more data meteorologists can collect about what is happening in the atmosphere, the better weather predictions they can make. The text explains, "This information helps meteorologists predict what kind of weather is headed our way." **3.** B; **4.** A; **5.** C; **6.** D; **7.** Students should complete the rubric to determine their level of

Answer Key

proficiency.

Assessment

Part 1: 1. The earthquake of 1906 caused massive damage in San Francisco. The text explains, "Walls fell, bridges and roads collapsed, and trees were uprooted." No part of the city was spared damage. **2.** San Francisco is likely to experience earthquakes because it lies on the San Andreas Fault. The text explains that this fault "is still the source of earthquakes today." Because it is on a fault, earthquakes are likely to happen in San Francisco. **3.** 1906, 5:12 A.M., 7.8, 30,000, 3,000

Part 2: 1. Some good may have come from the San Francisco earthquake of 1906. The city was rebuilt. "When the City Shook" explains that, "In many ways, the new city was better than before." After the quake, people probably built stronger buildings and made new rules for firefighters. After such a big quake, San Franciscans probably made changes to keep the city safer. **2.** The earthquake of 1906 was massive. The text states that, "San Francisco was nearly ruined." Families who had people living in the city at that time have probably passed down stories over the generations. Photographs and news articles from that time probably form an important part of the city's history.

Part 3: 1. Answers will vary. Possible answer: San Francisco city officials and services were unable to cope with the disaster. **2.** Answers will vary. Possible answers: As many as 50 fires broke out after the quake. Nearly 30,000 buildings were destroyed. About 3,000 people lost their lives. **3.** D

Part 4: 1. Roads and bridges were destroyed. Trees were uprooted, and soil particles lost contact with each other. Buildings collapsed and were burnt. City services such as water and firefighting were affected. About 3,000 people lost their lives. **2.** Answers will vary. Possible answers: Make buildings stronger. Train firefighters in how to stop fires from spreading. Build stronger water lines.

Part 5: 1. It is about the San Francisco earthquake of 1906. **2.** The earthquake was devastating. **3.** It happened in 1906. **4.** It happened in San Francisco along the San Andreas Fault. **5.** It is important to learn about natural disasters so we can try to protect ourselves in the future. **6.** Massive damage occurred to buildings, bridges, and water lines. People lost their lives. **7.** Summaries will vary. Possible summary: The San Francisco earthquake of 1906 was powerful and devastating. Buildings and bridges were destroyed, fires broke out, and people lost their lives. It is important to remember the damage that occurred so we can try to prevent it from happening again. This is especially important for San Franciscans who live along the San Andreas Fault where earthquakes are likely.